Spiral Draw

KLUTZ

TAKE THIS BOOK FOR A SPIN!

Fill it up with a zillion spirals.

TABLE OF CONTENTS

INTRODUCING

YOUR TOOLS

The Frame

This is the frame. Its job is to sit on
your drawing surface and go nowhere.
Sound cushy? It also has the important
job of keeping the drawing wheels
under control as they spin.

KLUTZ

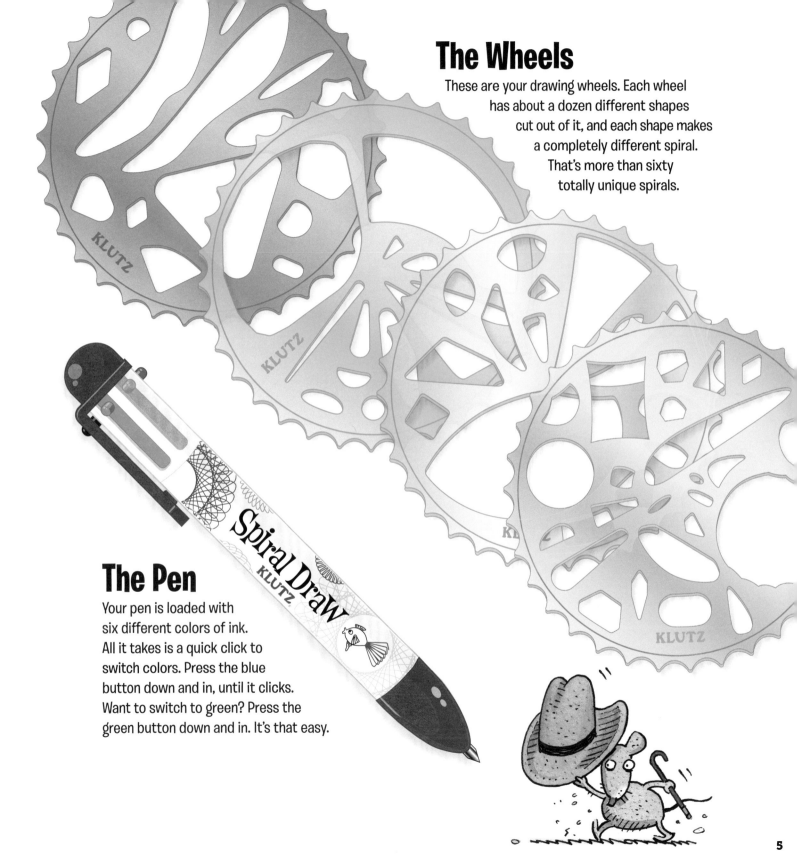

The Wheels

These are your drawing wheels. Each wheel has about a dozen different shapes cut out of it, and each shape makes a completely different spiral. That's more than sixty totally unique spirals.

The Pen

Your pen is loaded with six different colors of ink. All it takes is a quick click to switch colors. Press the blue button down and in, until it clicks. Want to switch to green? Press the green button down and in. It's that easy.

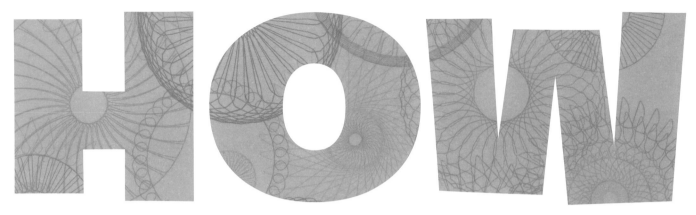

HOW

DO I DRAW WITH THIS STUFF?

Start with the wheel

Choose a wheel (any wheel) and lay it down on the next page so the word **KLUTZ** is face up.

Add the frame

Set the frame (also **KLUTZ**-side up) over the wheel. It will hold the wheel down against the paper.

Then, the pen

Hold the frame firmly in place with one hand, then put the pen in one of the cut-out shapes so the tip rests on the paper right up against the edge of the shape.

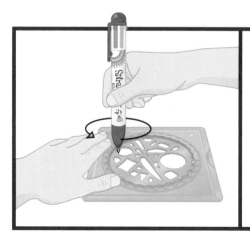

Now draw!

Trace the shape just like you're using a stencil. The pen will go around the shape, the wheel will spin around inside the frame, and your first spiral will appear. Keep drawing until you've made a complete round and your pen is back where it started.

We know you can't wait. Go ahead and make a spiral right now!

HOW DO I KNOW IF I GOT IT RIGHT?

 Right

 Right

 Really Right

Super Right

BiG

OR SMALL?

Small shapes close to the outside edge of the wheel make big, open spirals.

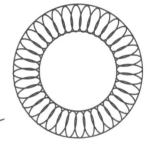

The closer the shape is to the center of the wheel, the smaller the spiral it will make.

Shapes that stretch from the outside of the wheel to the center make large, filled-in patterns.

KLUTZ

Make some BIG spirals!

Make some SMALL spirals!

SINGLES
THE START OF SOMETHING BIG

The spirals you've been making are called singles. They look great on their own, but more is almost always better.

String some singles together to make a chain.

Or pile them up on top of each other.

Singles Practice

Give this dog some
spiral Frisbees to catch.

STACKS

Make a stack by drawing two or more spirals around the same center. Stack up two spirals or ten. The more colors the better.

The easiest stack

Set up the wheel and frame as always, then make a complete spiral using any shape you like. Now — without moving the frame — make another spiral using a different shape. You'll end up with two neatly stacked, perfectly centered spirals.

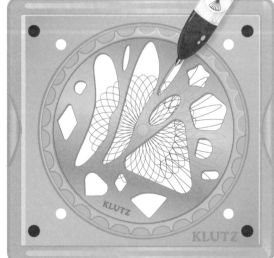

Fancy stacks

With just a little more effort, you can stack spirals made with different wheels.

Put the first wheel on your paper and cover it with the frame. Find the little holes in each corner of the frame and use a pencil to make a mark in each one (you can erase the marks later).

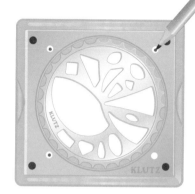

Draw your first spiral. It will be centered between the four marks.

Take the first wheel away and put the second one in its place. Make sure the frame's corner holes line up with the pencil marks you made. Switch to a new ink color and draw another spiral.

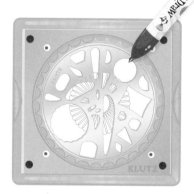

Make sure you can see the mark in each corner hole.

Erase your pencil marks and...

TA DA!

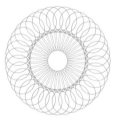

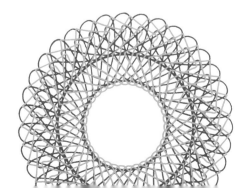

Stack Practice

Fill up this garden with stacked spirals.

You are now entering the
SPINZONE

On the following pages, complete the drawings with single spirals or stacks.

TIP:

No matter which shape in the wheel you use, the spiral will be centered in the frame.

SPIN ZONE

Spirals in Space

Make your own spiral galaxy.

Spiral Fireworks

Let spirals fill up the sky.

SPIN ZONE

Spiral Feathers

Give this peacock a colorful tail.

Up in the Air

Balance a bunch of spirals
on this seal's nose.

Way Up in the Air

Use spirals to keep this balloon afloat.

THE MEGAMARVELOUS MOUSTACHE MACHINE

Add spiral gears to this marvelous machine. The small shapes near the center of the wheels will work best.

BEFORE

MOUSTACHE HAIR

GLUE

MOLD

SPIN ZONE

26

Spiral
Surfing

Give this guy a spiral high tide to ride.

Spiral Sledding

Make a spiral mountain for this polar bear and his pals.

Spiral Butterfly

Fill this butterfly with colorful spirals.

SPIN ZONE

Spiral Fashion

Make a spiral tie-dye t-shirt.

You are now entering the...

DOODLE ZONE

Transform your decorative spirals into animals, people, and more.

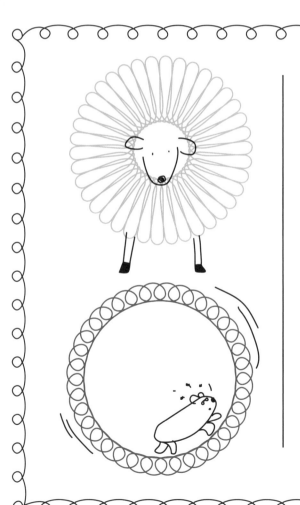

Adding a few doodles to complete spirals is great. But the real fun is found in

SEMI SPIRALS.

That's what you get when you stop a spiral, mid-spin.

BFEORE

AFTER

PURPLE SWIRLS BECOME...

...FEATHERS

ORANGE SWIRLS BECOME...

...RUNNING LEGS

THIS BECOMES...

...THIS

USE YOUR WHEELS AS STENCILS

SPIRAL DOODLE FISH

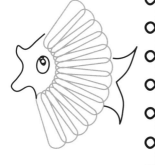

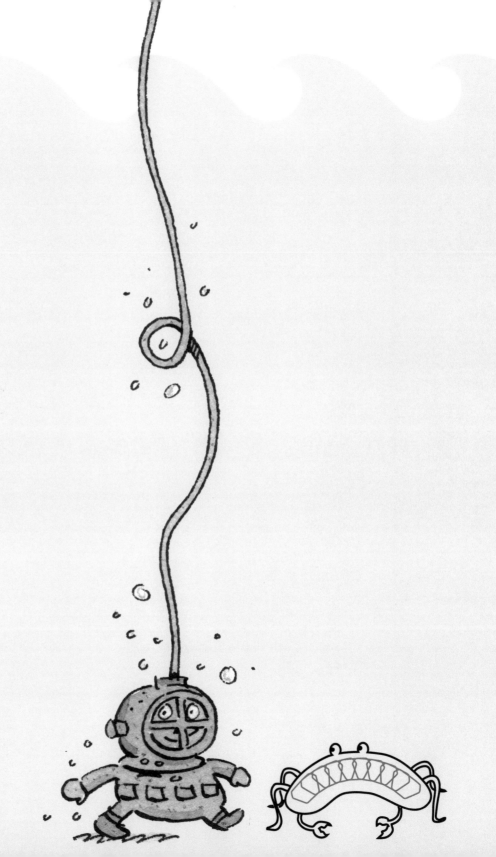

SPIRAL DOODLE BUGS

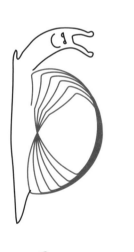

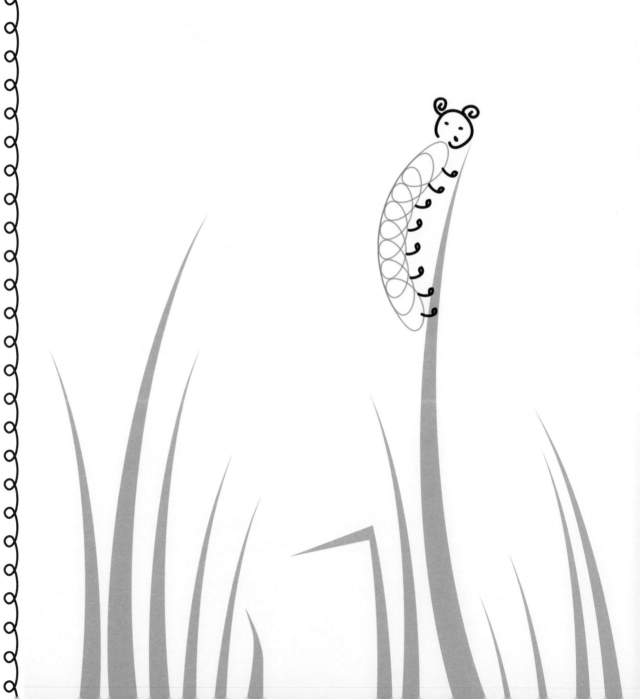

SPIRAL DOODLE BIRDS

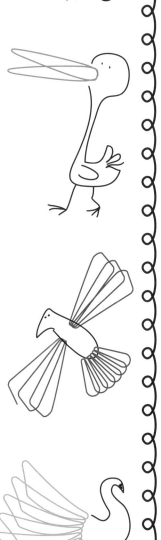

SPIRAL
DOODLE
DUEL

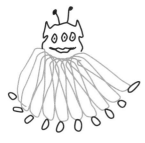

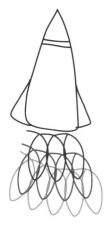

SPIRAL
DOODLE
DREAMS

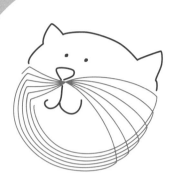

Make any spiral doodle.... off the top of your head.

Bad Hair Day

1 Fold the bottom corner of this page up as shown.

2 Draw a spiral that fills the blue circle. Unfold to reveal your spiral style.

GO OUT WITH A BANG!

Credits

Editors: Doug Stillinger, Michael Sherman, Kaitlyn Nichols, Anne Johnson

Designer: Kevin Plottner

Illustrators: Elwood Smith, Teshin Associates, Quillon Tsang, Sara Boore

Package Designer: David Avidor

Production Coordinators: Mimi Oey, Kelly Shaffer

Production Editor: Madeleine Robins

Thanks to David Barker, Liz Hutnick, Theresa Hutnick, Rebekah Lovato

Here are more Klutz books we think you'll like.